Interjections

Man!

Hey!

Eek!

Yikes!

Wow!

by Katie Marsico

CHERRY LAKE PUBLISHING · ANN ARBOR, MICHIGAN

CHERRY
LAKE
Publishing

A note on the text:
Certain words
are highlighted
as examples of
interjections.

Bold, colorful
words are
vocabulary words
and can be found
in the glossary.

Published in the United States of America by Cherry Lake Publishing
Ann Arbor, Michigan
www.cherrylakepublishing.com

Content Adviser: Lori Helman, PhD, Associate Professor, Department of
Curriculum & Instruction, University of Minnesota, Minneapolis, Minnesota

Photo Credits: Page 4, ©Cmlndm/Dreamstime.com; page 8,
©wavebreakmedia/Shutterstock, Inc.; page 10, ©Pete Pahham/
Shutterstock, Inc.; page 14, ©Pavel Losevsky/Dreamstime.com; page 16,
©Andresr/Shutterstock, Inc.; page 20, ©Rainer Plendl/Shutterstock, Inc.

Library of Congress Cataloging-in-Publication Data
Marsico, Katie, 1980–
  Interjections / By Katie Marsico.
    pages cm. — (Language Arts Explorer Junior)
  Includes bibliographical references and index.
  ISBN 978-1-62431-184-0 (lib. bdg.) — ISBN 978-1-62431-250-2
(e-book) — ISBN 978-1-62431-316-5 (pbk.)
1. English language—Interjections—Juvenile literature. I. Title.

  PE1355.M37 2013
  428.2–dc23   2013005087

Cherry Lake Publishing would like to acknowledge the work
of The Partnership for 21st Century Skills. Please visit www.p21.org
for more information.

Printed in the United States of America
Corporate Graphics Inc.
July 2013
CLFA13

Table of Contents

CHAPTER ONE

Whoa, Dinosaurs!

A huge dinosaur skeleton is the kind of thing that makes people say "wow!"

Will's mouth dropped open as soon as he and his sister, Lauren, walked into the museum. He was so excited that he wanted to jump up and down. Will and Lauren had been looking forward to seeing the museum's new *Tyrannosaurus rex* exhibit all week.

"Wow! That dinosaur skeleton is even more awesome than I imagined," Will said.

"Whoa! Check out the size of those bones!" Lauren shouted.

Will and Lauren were thrilled about having a chance to study a *T. rex* skeleton up close. They were also amazed by how big it was. Will's and Lauren's language showed their strong **emotions**. They used **interjections** such as *wow* and *whoa* when they talked.

Interjections are things people say when they are excited. They are **exclamations** that help **express** a speaker's thoughts and emotions. These words and **phrases** might show that a person agrees or disagrees with another statement. People also use interjections to **greet** others or when they are thinking of something to say.

A person does not always need to include interjections to get his or her point across. But these words and phrases help make speech and writing more lively. They bring out thoughts and feelings that add to the information that is being shared.

Yikes! T. rex is chasing me!

THINK ABOUT IT

Read and Rethink!

Carefully read the two conversations below. The first includes interjections. The second does not. What differences do you notice between the two?

CONVERSATION #1:

"Man!" Lauren said with a shiver. "That skeleton is cool, but, ooh, something about it gives me the creeps."

"Yep," agreed Will. "Hey, it almost reminds me of that horror movie where the *T. rex* was chasing those kids. I guess the real thing is pretty scary, huh?"

CONVERSATION #2:

"That skeleton is cool," Lauren said with a shiver. "But something about it gives me the creeps."

"It almost reminds me of that scary movie where the *T. rex* was chasing those kids," agreed Will. "I guess the real thing is pretty freaky."

CHAPTER TWO

A Look at Interjections

Wow! That's a large dinosaur!

"Hey! That *Tyrannosaurus rex* is bigger than our school bus," Will said. He was shocked when he realized this new fact. The word *hey* is one example of an interjection that speakers use to express surprise. So are terms such as *ah, whoa, wow, gosh,* and *oh.*

"Yikes! *T. rex* had super sharp teeth," said Lauren. The word *yikes* is an interjection that shows a speaker's fear. The term *eek* has the same effect.

"Uh-huh," said Will. "Those teeth must have been like razors." The interjections *uh-huh*, *sure*, *yep*, and *yes* express agreement. Speakers use interjections such as *no*, *no way*, and *nope* when they disagree with someone else.

THINK ABOUT IT

Extra Examples

Interjections express praise (bravo) and feelings of celebration (hooray and yippee) and happiness (ah). Speakers also use interjections to show disgust (ugh), frustration (darn and rats), and pain (ouch and ow).

"Hello there," said a museum worker as she walked up to Will and Lauren. "Do you two have any questions about our new *Tyrannosaurus rex* exhibit?" Speakers use interjections such as *hello*, *hey*, and *howdy* to greet other people. The phrases *bye*, *farewell*, and *good-bye* are a few other examples of interjections that serve to say good-bye.

You probably use an interjection such as *hi* or *hello* every time you answer the phone.

"Um, I think I have a question," answered Lauren. "Can you tell us exactly how many teeth *Tyrannosaurus rex* had?"

"Hmm, I'm not so sure you want to know the answer to that question, Lauren," laughed Will. "Do you remember how, uh, scared you got when the *T. rex* opened its mouth and showed all its pointy teeth during the movie we watched?" People sometimes use interjections such as *hmm*, *uh*, and *er* when they are thinking of what they want to say next. These words also express **hesitation** or **doubt**.

Hmm, I am not really sure.

ACTIVITY

Locate and List!

Wow, the museum is crowded today.

Locate and list all the interjections in the following paragraphs:

"Hi, guys," said a voice behind Will and Lauren. It was their friend Mia. "Wow, the museum is crowded today."

"Hello, Mia," answered Will. "Yep, I guess everyone wanted to check out the new dinosaur." Mia stared up at the skeleton in front of them.

"Whoa," she whispered. "That *T. rex* is pretty incredible, huh?"

To get a copy of this activity, visit www.cherrylakepublishing.com/activities.

"Yeah," said Lauren. "Gosh, just imagine if it was chasing you!"

"Eek!" shouted Mia. "Geez, knock it off, Lauren. I don't want to have nightmares!"

"OK," answered Lauren. "Hey, this lady works at the museum and was getting ready to tell us about all the teeth inside the mouth of a *T. rex*. Do you have a few seconds to stick around and hear what she has to say?"

"Darn!" said Mia. "I would love to learn more. I have to find my cousin and leave, though. Bye, you guys!"

Bye, Mia!

Answers: hi, wow, hello, yep, whoa, huh, yeah, gosh, eek, geez, OK, hey, darn, bye

CHAPTER THREE

Pay Attention to Punctuation!

Tyrannosaurus rex used its teeth to hunt and eat smaller dinosaurs. Yikes!

"Well," said the museum worker. "I don't want to scare your sister, Will. I do know the answer to your question though, Lauren. I believe *Tyrannosaurus rex* had about 60 teeth."

Interjections can be used with different kinds of **punctuation**. In the sentences on page 14 commas set interjections apart from other words in a phrase or sentence.

"Man!" shouted Lauren when she learned how many teeth the mighty *Tyrannosaurus rex* had.

"Phew!" said Will after thinking about what the museum worker had told them. "I sure am glad dinosaurs aren't alive anymore." In the sentences above exclamation marks follow interjections. They help show the strength of emotion interjections are expressing.

"Golly." Lauren stared at the museum worker. "Humans only have about 32 teeth, right?" Periods and question marks can come after interjections, too.

Speakers and writers use interjections to help show emotion, express a thought, or fill a pause. This may be at the beginning, middle, or end of a sentence. Interjections can also stand alone. When that happens, they are not part of a complete sentence.

People use interjections to express themselves when other words won't get the message across.

Extra Examples

Interjection used at the beginning of a sentence:
"Gee, that bug is tiny!"

Interjection used in the middle of a sentence:
"The answer to that math question is, uh, 90."

Interjection used at the end of a sentence:
"You like chocolate cake, huh?"

Interjection that stands alone:
"Whoops! I almost slipped in that puddle of juice in the middle of the floor."

So, what did you think of T. rex?

"Phooey!" cried Lauren as she checked her watch. "I was paying so much attention to our talk about *T. rex* teeth that I forgot we need to get home, Will."

"Aw, darn," her brother said. "How about we stay just a few more minutes, Lauren?"

"Nope," replied Lauren. "I promise that we will come back soon though, OK?"

"Bye," said Will to the museum worker. "Boy, we learned a lot today."

"Yup," said Lauren. "Oh, well. I guess it's time we head back to tell Mom and Dad a few facts about dinosaurs. Farewell, *Tyrannosaurus rex*!"

You must have learned a lot, huh?

Wow, we sure did!

STOP!
DON'T WRITE IN THE BOOK!

THINK ABOUT IT

Read and Rethink!

Read the conversation below. Then rewrite it by adding punctuation to the interjections.

"Hey Mom and Dad," yelled Will. "Boy did Lauren and I have a good time!"

"Goodness gracious You two are excited," said Mom.

"You must have seen something pretty amazing huh" asked Dad.

Answers:

"Hey, Mom and Dad," yelled Will. "Boy, did Lauren and I have a good time!"

"Goodness gracious! You two are excited," said Mom.

"You must have seen something pretty amazing, huh?" asked Dad.

To get a copy of this activity, visit www.cherrylakepublishing.com/activities.

People do not rely on interjections only when talking about dinosaur exhibits at a museum. Speakers and writers use interjections every day in all kinds of situations. These words and phrases show what a person is thinking and feeling.

How will you use interjections to spice up your writing?

They serve as greetings and pauses in conversation. Interjections help make language come alive!

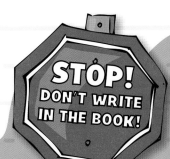

THINK ABOUT IT

Read and Rethink!

Read the following conversation between Will and Lauren. Rewrite what they say to each other by filling in the blanks with interjections:

"_____!" said Will. "This ad in the newspaper says that the museum will be getting three new dinosaur exhibits next month. _____, should we go back and look at those skeletons, too?"

   "_____," answered Lauren. "_____, I cannot wait to learn about other dinosaurs besides *Tyrannosaurus rex*. Do you think they will be as scary as the skeleton we saw today?"

   "_____," said Will. "I doubt anything is as scary as *T. rex* bones. Yet there's only one way to find out, _____?"

To get a copy of this activity, visit www.cherrylakepublishing.com/activities.

Glossary

doubt (DOUT) the state of being uncertain about something

emotions (i-MO-shuhnz) feelings

exclamations (ek-skluh-MAY-shuhnz) sudden statements that usually show the speaker's strong feelings

express (ik-SPRES) to share thoughts or feelings

greet (GREET) to welcome someone as he or she arrives

hesitation (hez-uh-TAY-shuhn) when someone pauses because he or she is unsure of something

interjections (in-tur-JEK-shuhnz) words or phrases used to express emotions or pauses in speech

phrases (FRAY-ziz) expressions made up of one or more words

punctuation (puhngk-chu-WAY-shuhn) the marks used to separate words and sentences

For More Information

BOOK

Cleary, Brian P. *Cool! Whoa! Ah and Oh!: What Is an Interjection?*
Minneapolis: Millbrook Press, 2011.

WEB SITE

BrainPOP—Interjections

www.brainpop.com/english/grammar/interjections/preview.weml
Watch a cartoon that explains interjections.

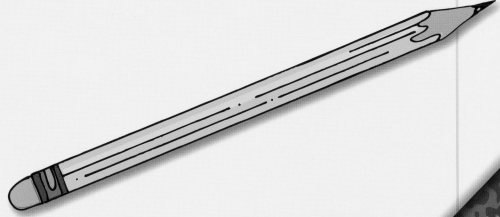

Index

About the Author

Katie Marsico is an author of children's and young-adult reference books. She lives outside of Chicago, Illinois, with her husband and children.